CATNIP
and
KEROSENE GRASS

What Plants Teach Us About Life

by

Gina Mohammed, PhD

Drawings by Nathalie Gagné

Candlenut Books
Sault Ste. Marie, Ontario, Canada
www.CandlenutBooks.com

CATNIP AND KEROSENE GRASS
What Plants Teach Us About Life

Published in Canada by:

Candlenut Books
66 Millwood Street
Sault Ste. Marie, Ontario
P6A 6S7

www.CandlenutBooks.com

National Library of Canada Cataloguing in Publication

Mohammed, Gina H
    Catnip and kerosene grass : what plants teach us about life / by Gina Mohammed ; drawings by Nathalie Gagné.

ISBN 0-9731097-0-X

1. Inspiration. 2. Happiness. 3. Peace of mind. 4. Conduct of life. 5. Plants. I. Gagné, Nathalie, 1989- II. Title.

BF632.M64 2002   158.1   C2002-902754-3

In Memory
of
Pappy

(who stubbornly called
every flower a Rose)

Papala Tree
Life's sparkle

The papala tree grows in Hawaii, where the natives have taken advantage of its high inflammability to make a form of amusement for themselves. Carving spears out of the soft wood of the tree, they set them afire and launch them skyward from the edges of tall cliffs. The dazzling spears glide across the sky, making a wonderful display of fireworks for onlookers in their canoes below, and sailing considerable distances on the trade winds before settling into the sea.

Life isn't meant to provide a continuous whirl of flash and excitement – just a few well-placed sparks to brighten our horizon, sail the trade winds of our memory, and leave a perfect afterglow in our hearts.

Arctic Poppy
Magnify your talent

Arctic poppies have delicate flowers that are shaped like parabolic cups. This shape allows them to concentrate the rays from the sun, thereby creating an inviting chamber of yellow light that entices insect pollinators. It is a cunning plant, indeed, that can take the same ration of sunlight as another plant and enhance it to such brilliance.

It's that way with people too. Those who shine brightest are simply those who have learned how to multiply and enhance their share of talent. They mold their characters, habits, and attitudes to make the most of what they have been given. And the result is often what we call genius.

Olive
Don't let age stop you

The olive tree is a rich source of valuable food, oil, and wood. It has a fine history too, for in biblical times, Jesus visited the Garden of Gethsemane at the Mount of Olives to pray. It is possible that some of the olive trees there today were present at that time, since they can live more than 1500 years.

An unusual feature of this tree is its ability to fruit in very old age – even at 700 hundred years old! A second special trait is that it can renew itself from decay and destruction of shoots and roots by simply sprouting new ones.

When I think of the olive tree, I am reminded that any limits that arise as I get older are largely self-imposed. We can be as productive and useful as we wish to be, at any age. Learn a new skill, vary your routine, make a new friend.

Coral Reef
Work with others

Coral reefs are breathtaking jewels of vibrant colour adorning the tropical seas. The reef is really a hard protective material secreted by the soft-bodied corals living inside. But these little animals do not work alone. Their reefs are home to special algae which, in exchange for shelter and nutrients, make sugar and protein that the corals desperately need. Together, these partners – so dissimilar in nature – make possible each other's survival and growth.

And so it is with us. Working with others very different from ourselves, we surpass our limitations, and create legacies together that survive the passage of time. Seek out colleagues with abilities different than your own, even if it makes you uncomfortable at first. Then witness the miracles possible in diversity.

Poplar
Focus your energy

The poplar family is adept at tough living, thriving in harsh northern winters and near-barren lands. One of its secrets – and one shared by many northern plants – is that it focuses its energies and emphasizes one thing at a time. It concentrates either on growing roots, or leaves, or stem, as dictated by the time of year. It doesn't dissipate its strength trying to do everything all at once. And in autumn, deciduous trees such as the poplar readily relinquish their leaves, thereby avoiding branch breakage from the weight of heavy snow. The capacity to focus is crucial to the poplar's survival, allowing it to make the most of its limited resources.

If we could focus on one thing at a time and do it well, how much more peace, energy, and satisfaction we would have. We could enjoy a sense of accomplishment instead of merely stumbling from task to task. And if we could relinquish excess paraphernalia, perhaps we could better absorb the strain of life's twists and turns. In today's challenging world, we have a great advantage if we can simplify and focus.

Cork Oak
Resilience

Cork is a familiar product. Good quality cork comes from the cork oak tree, a tall evergreen that grows in Mediterranean countries such as Spain and Portugal. Although most types of trees have a layer of cork directly under the outer bark, the cork oak is a particularly prolific producer of this material.

To obtain cork, the outer bark is peeled from the tree every 8 to 15 years, but this doesn't kill or permanently harm the tree as long as the inner bark layer is left intact. The cork oak simply replenishes itself and regrows a fresh supply of cork. Good cork may be formed by some trees for as long as 200 years. The cork oak is a resilient tree and produces a valuable, durable product that is used in so many articles – bottle stoppers, net floats, life preservers, artificial limbs, flooring, and insulation, to name but a few.

As with the cork oak, persistence and ability to recover in the face of loss marks our quality as individuals. Moreover, a resilient person invariably bears exceptional fruit, fertilized by strength of character. When we think of the buoyancy of cork, let us also remember to cultivate a similarly buoyant spirit.

Islaya Cactus
Test your talents

The Islaya cactus grows in the Pacific coast deserts of South America. It's an unusual habitat, often having no rainfall for years at a time. The cacti lie nestled in the sandy or stony desert without any roots at all, staying alive only through the mists from the nearby sea. Yet, even small seedlings eventually manage to produce lovely yellow flowers the size of silver dollars. The Islaya obviously does not let its lack of roots stop it from achieving the remarkable.

How often do we hesitate to pursue our dreams because we feel deficient in talent, knowledge, or experience – the perceived roots of success. But chances are that we carry untapped strengths and abilities which, when enfolded within the mist of optimism, can conspire to accomplish marvellous things.

Teddy Bear Cholla
Be yourself

The chollas are the prickliest members of the cactus family. And, the teddy bear cholla is the prickliest of all. A small desert shrub, the teddy bear mimics its namesake by virtue of its numerous closely-packed prickles that, from a distance, look like fluffy white fur glistening in the bright desert sun. But brush close to the teddy bear, and it soon becomes evident that there's nothing cuddly about this plant. The spines stick fast to the flesh, coming off not one-by-one but in clusters. A deceptive little shrub – harmless in appearance, but fierce in deportment.

Yet this ornery shrub is home to certain animals, such as the cactus wren and the pack rat, who make good use of its thorny accommodation for nesting and protection from predators. These critters, for some reason, get along just fine with the teddy's prickly disposition.

We often present to the world an image that is deceptive. To impress and attract others, we tend to show teddy bear attributes. And, while there's nothing wrong with sharing our softer side, we should never pretend it's all that we are. Eventually we can't help but show our true selves, and then it may be too late to keep those we have sought to win. Friends worth keeping are those who see all sides of you and love you anyway. We don't have to please everyone.

Oregano
Life in context

Oregano oil may be an excellent antibiotic. Researchers have found that it fights *Staphylococcus* bacteria as successfully as the standard antibiotics penicillin, streptomycin, and vancomycin. (*Staph* bacteria have become increasingly resistant to conventional antibiotics in recent years.) Best of all, oregano oil appears to work at low doses. It is possible that carvacrol, a key ingredient in the oil, is responsible for this action.

Interestingly, however, when carvacrol is used alone or with another oil carrier such as olive oil, there is virtually no antibiotic effect. Apparently, the benefit resides in the broader makeup of the oil, rather than in this one component exclusively. On its own, carvacrol may lose the context in which to act most effectively.

Context is a marvellous and necessary thing. But don't we often try to inspect life's pieces out of context, and then wonder why they don't make sense or why they don't work as well as we expect? Some pieces of life may be appreciated only when seen in the light of another part – perhaps a part that you have not yet lived.

Wormwood
Target the weak spots

The bitter herb wormwood has a history of use as a medicinal plant among certain cultures. It may even hold promise as a cancer treatment. One of the chemicals in wormwood, called artemisinin, apparently kills cancer cells while leaving healthy ones alone. It does so by reacting with iron to produce damaging free radicals, iron being abundant in cancer cells to drive their proliferation. Researchers found that iron-rich cancer cells exposed to artemisinin died within hours.

Artemisinin kills cancer by targeting its weakness. Is there something in your life that's akin to a cancer? Something that wearies you and hinders your serenity and progress? It's easy to be overwhelmed and want to give up. Instead, look for the vulnerable places of that cancer. What does it depend on to flourish at your expense – a mind set, a fear, or even a misguided ambition? Tackle the beast on that point, mounting a selective campaign that will destroy the problem for good.

Old Man Cactus
Be patient

The Old Man Cactus is familiar to cacti lovers, with its long wavy hair, akin to the silvery-white beard of an elderly gentleman. This plant is fond of heat, sun, drought, and poor soil. In these conditions, it grows slowly – as little as a foot in a decade. It does not produce flowers or fruit until it is about 20 feet tall.

It seems these plants are never in a hurry. Their time for blossoming will come eventually, and they are content to wait for it – doing so under conditions most of us would not find particularly pleasant.

Would many of us be ready to wait until we are old to have our day? Or are we too busy rushing to squeeze a lifetime of magic into a second or two of the present? Fulfilment is allowing life to unfold in its own time, with patience and with grace.

Lichen
Sustenance for the future

L ichens are an amazing partnership between fungi and algae, the one providing support and structure, the other nutrients and sustenance. Lichens can live several hundred years on trees and in harsh habitats such as wind-ravaged mountain rocks. They even adapt happily to life on graveyard tombstones. They draw nutrients from dew and rainfall, and store the food in their bodies for very long periods, releasing nourishment gradually as needed. The lichen can thus sustain itself almost indefinitely in a tough environment.

What provisions do you need to sustain you tomorrow? A certain amount of food, money, clothing, and household goods are only a start. What about the sustenance that comes from family, friendships, and sound values? It's never too soon to stock your storehouse with these treasures that nourish over a lifetime.

Jack Pine
Benefit from trials

No one likes trials. Trials introduce delays, frustrations, grief, and, sometimes, a sense of failure in our lives. But we often don't realize that trials can yield great benefits.

I think of the example provided by the jack pine. This forest tree grows in fire-prone areas of the north, where a blaze can devastate a stand in short order. Yet the jack pine ultimately thrives specifically because of fire – its seed cones are encased in a thick wax coating and the seeds can be released only following exposure to intense heat. So the jack pine needs the fire to reproduce and endure through time.

When you encounter your next fiery trial, try to focus on the benefits instead of the heat. Look for the lessons, and treat your burden as a weight-training exercise that will build muscle, strength, and endurance. You'll go from trial to triumph.

Walking Fern
Be surefooted

Plants aren't supposed to get up and move around, but it seems no one has ever informed the walking fern. Living on shady outcrops of moss-blanketed limestone, the walking fern is a beautiful plant, its elegant sunbursts of slender lance-shaped leaves gracefully arching across the emerald carpets. And where a leaf tip touches the ground, it forms a rooted plantlet which then extends its own fronds to continue the march. To an observer it appears to walk – slowly but surely, sprouting new plants at each step, in time producing quite a community of flourishing plants.

How do you walk through your life? Are your steps surefooted, or are they tentative? If tentative, maybe you need to root your steps in something of lasting value. Without it, your actions run out of steam and your progress is soon halted. Surefootedness comes when each step of the way is solidly planted and rooted before the next step is taken. It is the only way to advance and flourish.

Carob
True value

The carob is a small evergreen tree that grows in fertile regions of the Mediterranean. Its seeds, being rich in protein, are ground into a health-food flour that is used in baking.

But the interesting thing about this tree is that, because of their remarkably uniform weight, the hard carob seeds (known as carats in ancient times) were used as standards to assess the worth of precious metals and gemstones. Today, diamonds are still measured in carats, and pure gold is said to be "24 karats".

It's heartening to know that something as precious as gold or diamonds can be weighed against something so humble as a tree seed. It reminds us that no thing or person is ever too great to dodge the weight of simple standards. Gentleness, faithfulness, kindness, self-control – these are some of the measures that certify 24-karat character.

Algae
Rest when you can

These days it is a common thing for people to get too little rest. We live harried lives and seem to have no time to just relax and renew ourselves. When stressful times come, our reserves are already drained and we can be nudged over the edge.

In the plant world, rest – deep rest – is a given. Consider the various types of algae that inhabit harsh areas such as the Antarctic and Death Valley. In such extreme climates, algae cannot always grow and reproduce. When it is too cold, too hot, or too dry, algae go to sleep – a deep sleep that can last months, or even years. They make no food and stop growing. They even stop aging, virtually suspended in time. When the weather improves, they wake up and carry on.

During times of personal stress, do we try to keep running, sometimes in circles, draining what reserves we have? Or do we build rest into these times? It almost seems counterintuitive to rest when we think we should act. But we may be doing more harm than good by our frenzied efforts. From those times of rest, our inner strength can be renewed, our thoughts properly focused, and our actions rendered more effective.

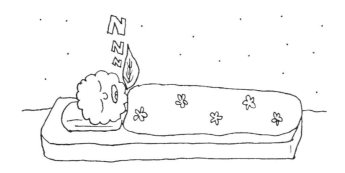

Venus Fly Trap
Trapped by the little things

The Venus fly trap is a well-known carnivorous plant that captures unsuspecting bugs wandering into its trap. Contained in its two fan-shaped lobes are a total of six tiny sensory hairs. When a bug enters the trap and nudges these little hairs, it activates a network of electrical communications in the plant that causes the lobes to quickly clamp shut – to the detriment of the hapless insect. The plant then digests its prey, extracting nitrogen and other nutrients it needs to survive.

If the prey never touched those little hairs, it would get out alive and well. The hairs look harmless and they're so tiny. But their size belies their power. Indirectly, these structures ensnare and, ultimately, kill.

Be on the lookout for the Venus fly traps in your life. Those traps contain tiny, inconspicuous killers – small, apparently harmless things that we don't think too much about because they appear so manageable. It may be a pet habit, a behaviour, or an attitude that may just end up betraying us.

Water Lily
Anchor yourself

L ike china teacups balanced on emerald saucers, water lilies grace the surface of ponds and stream edges everywhere. These serene flowers provide both beauty to our eyes and a landing site for small birds. They are a source of food for wildlife and people.

Lilies appear to abide effortlessly on the water's surface. And that's almost true, except for the fact that they are firmly planted in the ground beneath. Thick anchorage roots, several feet long in places, run from the flower and leaf all the way to the bottom. Channels in these thick roots serve as oxygen pipelines that aerate the submerged parts, and there are finer feeder roots with many hairs and a high surface area for nutrient absorption.

We don't think of this intricate support network when we look at a water lily. All we see is a flower and pad floating on the water, as if by magic. But without its anchorage and feeder system, the water lily would wither and die. Serenity and real beauty cannot endure unless they are solidly anchored in a healthy foundation, one that plumbs the full depth of our soul.

Cannonball Tree
The confidence to be different

The cannonball tree is found in the jungles of the Amazon and other tropical settings. And what an oddball tree it is. It produces round brown fruits, iron-hard and up to 8 inches around, which mature and drop with a thud to the forest floor (or onto the head of a hapless victim). In parks where cannonball trees are grown as ornamentals, one can find prominent signs warning visitors of the falling fruit. Within these fruit are small white seeds in an unpleasant-smelling jelly. By contrast, the flowers of the cannonball tree have a heavenly scent, likened to a fine perfume. These flowers are produced in a rather unusual location for a tree – on thick woody extensions sprouting directly from the trunk – and they cascade down in large numbers. These will be the future cannonballs.

Oddities are commonplace in nature, and thankfully so, as they spice our world with delightful sprinkles of humour and surprise. One wonders... if plants are treasured for their rather oddball ways, why are people so often held to dull conformity? Our idiosyncrasies define who we really are. So enjoy your quirks, and let the rest of the world worry about figuring you out.

Bromeliads
What are you hoarding?

Bromeliads, a family of plants found mainly in tropical America, generally grow on host trees. Their appearance is slightly reminiscent of the common pineapple, which is a member of the family. Many tree-borne bromeliads possess upturned leaves that are broad at the bases, forming cup-like reservoirs to collect rainwater, dust, animal droppings, dead or decomposing insects, and other bits of debris that fall or blow into it. This unappetizing-sounding mixture actually makes a nutritious soup that sustains the plant (as well as small insects, spiders, and scorpions) over the dry season.

In a way, these plants remind me of people who love to accumulate odds and ends. You know... the clutterbugs who never throw anything out. Their basements, garages, sheds, and offices are stuffed to overflowing with remnants of this and that – items that may come in handy one day. Or mementos of childhood, adolescence, and every other age – things that take space to store, energy to maintain, and money to move. But unlike the case of bromeliads, much of what is hoarded is actually of very little value.

Retain only that which is helpful: a hearty soup to strengthen you and others during times of need, sadness, or discouragement. Anything else is simply not worth keeping.

Roses and Garlic

Companions

One doesn't usually associate the heavenly-scented rose with the pungent, earthy garlic bulb – two opposites indeed in the plant world. But strangely enough, this unlikely pair make fantastic companion plants.

Roses are a favourite of aphids and they are commonly ravaged by black spot disease, both sources of challenge and frustration to gardeners. But introduce a few garlic plants around the root of the rose, and pests are promptly kept in check. Gardeners have demonstrated that roses grown with garlic do far better than those without.

Strange? Perhaps not. Roses are a little like people in this way, gaining from the companionship of another whose natural abilities and personality complement rather than mimic their own. Instead of the spirit of competition that often mars the relationships of similar people, our opposites may be able to cultivate the best that's in us. So remember the roses and garlic, and reach out to different kinds of people – it will surely enrich your life.

Divi-Divi
Check your compass

The divi-divi tree is Aruba's natural compass. In sheltered spots, the tree is symmetrical with a spreading mounded top, but under the influence of steady trade winds that blow across the island from the northeast, the divi-divi bends sharply in the opposite direction – thus always pointing to the southwest. It's quite a sight to see these lopsided thirty-foot trees like elongated fingers directing your path.

Just as the trade wind re-orients the divi-divi, so too the winds of our times can sway and lock us into positions of unnatural strain and stress. Pressures to compete, acquire, and succeed thwart a balanced state of mind and set us in directions that are dangerously off target. Perhaps it's time to check your compass.

Sedge
Cushion your walk

In some areas of the world where the land is very wet and people routinely tread through bogs and marshes, natives have devised creative methods of keeping their feet dry and comfortable. For instance, in Lapland, a tradition is to line boots with fine sedge that grows along the edges of marshes. The sedge is beaten and dried, then packed carefully into the boot. With a cozy sedge lining, feet stay warm and comfortable no matter what – which would be impossible with regular socks. If the sedge gets wet, it's removed and simply hung on a stick near a fire to dry out in a few minutes. It can then be reworked and remolded by folding it around the fist and slipping it back into the boot. Thus outfitted, one can continue along the way.

Luxuries aren't always the things we've come to expect – the stately homes, prestigious automobiles, cruise vacations, and costly jewels. They are the things that cushion our daily walk and give us respite from our troubles. They are simple and plentiful if we know where to look and how to enjoy them. They are the moments of stillness, the kind word given and received, and the pleasure of a good laugh. These offer a renewable, resilient insulation to soften the day.

Haleakala Silversword
Your efforts matter

The craters of dormant Hawaiian volcanoes are not the most enviable of growing environments for plants. Rather miserable, dry, and dull to be sure. But, nestled on the volcanic mounds of the flat crater floors, a special plant can be found. The Haleakala silversword is a round moon-coloured plant, as large as a bushel basket, that lives for 20 years. Right before it dies, it puts out a spectacular six-foot flower stalk with masses of rich purple blooms. This final show of beauty seems sad in a way, rather wasted on the hidden volcanic floor.

But who can say that such an effort in an obscure place is for nothing? Someone had to see that beauty to report it to the rest of the world. And even if no one ever beheld this lovely plant, it will have served its purpose – to grow and make provision for another generation.

You might feel that your own energies are being wasted in a forgotten corner of life, or your finest effort may seem unimportant when compared to what you see others do. But if it is your best and it is done for an honourable reason, it will have its effect. And it will be appreciated in a special way by those who matter.

Pingwing
Opportunities

The pingwing plant inhabits the deeply shaded rainforest floors of Central America. It can function in that dark environment because it knows how to take advantage of sudden brief flickers of light that find their way to the forest floor. The pingwing quickly captures these sunflecks to provide itself with energy essential for survival and growth. Thus it thrives in an environment where it might otherwise be overtaken by larger plants that seize most of the sunshine.

The pingwing has mastered an important skill: It can recognize an opportunity and wastes no time acting upon it. In doing so, it ensures a place for itself in a very competitive world.

We each are presented with opportunities and the unique abilities to make the most of them. But be ready to act – a sunfleck could be focusing on you at this very moment.

Acacia
A humble start

Acacia – native to much of Africa and the Middle East – has an unusual means of regeneration: Rather than relying on seed dispersal by wind, they are particularly well-adapted to dispersal by elephant droppings. Unless the seeds pass through the elephant's alimentary canals, they are unlikely to germinate. No one really knows why this works so well, but it's been speculated that it might have something to do with the action of digestive acids on the seed coat. A casual observer can see tiny acacias sprouting merrily and producing little pea-shaped leaves atop a generous banquet of dried elephant stools.

This seems such a lowly beginning for a tree that is one of the few great timber species of the Arabian deserts, especially one that may well have provided the wood for the biblical Ark of the Covenant. But it shows that great things are often nurtured in the humblest of beginnings. And in the humblest of hearts.

Naupaka
Futile escapades

There is a legend about the naupaka flower, which grows in the Hawaiian Islands. The flower has five petals, but their arrangement looks like it's meant to have six and one has been plucked from the top. As the legend goes, two lovers had a quarrel, and the young lady grabbed the flower and tore it apart. Then she presented it to her young man and said she would have nothing more to do with him unless he located a perfect specimen for her. The unfortunate fellow searched high and low but, alas, could not find the perfect six-petalled flower, and ended up dying of a broken heart.

Legends usually tell us something about ourselves. This one points to the futility of our preoccupations. Sometimes we are obsessed with searching high and low for something that never was and was never meant to be. And why do we do it? Perhaps for the love of something or someone that is not right for us. But why we do it is not what matters – only that we stop before it destroys us.

Johnny Jump-Ups
Make room for others

Johnny jump-ups keep popping up in my yard. Years ago we planted one or two. Now I can't get rid of them. They seed and re-seed, spreading from flower garden to vegetable patch, lawn, and rockery. Multiplying wildly, this pansy quickly forms a thick mass of small purple and white flowers – rather pretty, but a nuisance eventually.

The thing that amazes me about these flowers is how well they seem to keep other plants away. Even weeds are intimidated by their presence. They seem harmless enough, but something about them deters neighbouring plants from getting too close. Other kinds of plants are like that too, producing toxins, hogging the light, or crowding out the roots of other plants.

Johnny jump-ups remind me of some people – those individuals who have a way of keeping others at arm's length, even alienating them. It may be through gossip that poisons, an overbearing manner that suffocates, or a self-centeredness that covets the spotlight. They crowd out everyone else and eventually end up with only themselves for company.

Liana
Be flexible

When we think of tropical jungle plants, we envision giant-leafed vegetation, riotously coloured blooms, towering old trees, and thick hanging rope-like vines or lianas. Some have exotic names such as monkey ladder and water vine.

Lianas are strong woody vines that root in the ground. Lacking their own tree trunks, they wind themselves around, across, and up large tropical trees, eventually reaching the top of the forest canopy and the sunlight. Once in the light, lianas sprout luxuriant leaves and flowers. En route, they have grown in many directions, entwining into knots, braids, and circles, in a seemingly circuitous journey. But these twists and turns result from a great flexibility in responding to local environmental changes, allowing lianas to continue their upward climb, eventually reaching their goal.

Aren't our journeys so often like that? Twists and turns in our lives are seen as fruitless delays and hindrances instead of stepping stones to a richer future. The knots, braids, and circles that we so resist and resent should instead be embraced with a spirit of flexibility, for flexibility does not diminish our purpose – rather, it assures its fulfilment.

Victoria Amazonica Lily
Strength

A grand flower of the Amazon is the Victoria Amazonica, a giant lily whose pad easily grows to six feet wide with 12-inch flowers. Each lily is supported from below by an immense network of hollow ribs protected by long sharp spines. Large and strong enough to support the weight of nesting birds or even a small animal or person, this lily is a marvel of strength and balance.

The Amazonica lily is reputed to be the inspiration behind the famous Crystal Palace, the Great Exhibition Hall of the first World's Fair in 1851. Designed and built by a botanist named Joseph Paxton, the building covered 23 acres! Modelled after the lily, the Crystal Palace had a skeleton of hollow iron ribs, arranged radially and strengthened by slender cross ribs to produce a light airy structure with wide open spaces. Like the flower, it was an awesome sight to behold.

Great strength is not associated, as many would believe, with brute force and a heavy-handed demeanour. Nor is it the product of a vast quantity of anything. Inevitably, strength proceeds from an inner network of finely-honed supports that ingeniously serve to anchor and yet uplift, to contain and yet promote growth.

Alpine Phlox
Stay energized

The tundra is an inhospitable environment. Yet the alpine phlox does just fine there. Forming an inconspicuous mound of tiny leaves and small white flowers, a 150-year-old alpine phlox may grow no larger than a baseball. It is a conservative plant – slow-growing and energy-efficient – yet, amazingly, its compactness allows it to maintain a temperature inside the mound about 20 degrees warmer than its cold environment. Now that's a plant with fire in its belly!

Of course, we also are apt to get ourselves all heated up. But sometimes that heat builds and builds until it gets the better of us, and we explode in a fiery tantrum. Rather than using our energy for warmth and growth, we waste it – and usually do harm in the process. How much healthier to stay quiet, controlled, and totally energized.

Chicory
Simple pleasures

In North America, by the roadsides and waste places, an eye-catching wildflower called chicory emerges in midsummer. I always anticipate its appearance around my neighbourhood, its blue daisy-like flowers gracing the roadside as I drive by. But chicory is more than just pretty. Its roots have been roasted and used since Napoleon's time as a coffee substitute, and today, ground chicory is an ingredient in some coffee blends.

Chicory differs from coffee in that it lacks caffeine and caffeotannic acid, and contains a great deal of ash and silica. When infused, it gives coffee a bitterish taste and a dark colour. Some say it counteracts the stimulation caused by coffee. Chicory can be a satisfying alternative for those who want to – but can't – drink coffee.

Life's pleasures don't have to be complicated, costly, or restricted to cultivated tastes. They can often be found by the wayside. But how easy to overlook them as we hurry along the road to someplace else.

Artist's Conk
Legacies

The artist's conk is a special type of fungus that forms a bracket-shaped plate on hardwood forest trees. Its underside is a flat white surface which discolours when touched. A line or drawing etched into the surface will almost immediately turn brown and will be preserved for a long time once the surface has dried. Many artists – and would-be artists – have created small masterpieces on the canvas of the artist's conk. One old-timer who drew a likeness of his log cabin claims it was still preserved even after 40 years!

The curious thing about the artist's conk is that it is found only on dead, dying, or severely stressed trees. Its presence on a tree is an almost sure sign that the tree will not live. The fungus doesn't kill the tree, but colonizes it once the tree's doom has been sealed.

The legacy of your life may not be a great achievement or superior success. It may simply be the support you've provided to another whose completed canvas will be your finest eulogy – someone you helped perhaps when you were having tough times in your own life.

Saguaro Cactus
Shape up for growth

The saguaro is the most majestic of cacti. Found only in the Sonoran Desert, it is a colossus of strength and solidity. Saguaros have been known to live for 200 years, attaining a height of 50 feet and a root spread of a hundred feet. Its character is ideally suited to the parched sands of the Sonoran, where water visits very infrequently.

When there is a "wet" summer, the saguaro sponges up enough moisture to expand its width as much as 50%, then releases the stored water frugally over a year or two of subsequent drought. It accommodates the massive influx of water by way of a flexible multi-ridged skin, which stretches and shrinks accordion-like as needed. The elastic nature of the saguaro's body equips it well for immediate storage and future growth.

We also benefit from a certain elasticity in our nature. For the mind that refuses to absorb new ideas eventually starves; and the spirit that does not shape itself to accommodate growth eventually perishes in a desert of its own creation.

Oak
Don't clog your system

Oak trees can be infected by a nasty disease called bacterial leaf scorch. Leaves on diseased trees begin to dry along their edges. Then death progresses slowly to the middle of the leaf and down the stem, into the branches and eventually to the trunk. Caused by a bacterium that colonizes and physically clogs the tree's water-conducting tissues (the xylem), bacterial leaf scorch causes great disruption of water movement in the tree because of massive numbers of multiplying bacteria and their by-products. The presence of the bacteria also triggers a defensive reaction that further plugs the xylem, thereby worsening the problem and eventually killing the tree.

We are all beset by problems at one time or another. These seem to infect our lives, clog our thinking, and strangle our peace of mind. But let's be careful not to make the situation worse by over-reacting. A tendency to dwell too much on the problem and neglect other areas of life can overload our system – both mentally and physically – and secure our demise. Keep those problems contained in a manageable package.

Opium Poppy
Keep money in its place

Chemicals from the opium poppy are well known for their euphoric and pain-suppressing qualities. Various alkaloids are present in the plant, morphine being one of the most important from a medical standpoint. Morphine can suppress pain, but it can also induce hallucinations. It is chemically related to the endorphins, which are produced by the human endocrine system and can trigger pain-reducing and euphoric effects.

Morphine is highly addictive, and high doses can cause death. Its therapeutic use as a pain reliever is carefully controlled so that it doesn't become a killer. Lethality is but a matter of degree.

There are other aspects of life where the distinction between help and harm is but a matter of degree. Our attitude to money is one. It's nice to have enough for the necessities of life and some of the extras. But, as with a narcotic drug, we may become addicted, eventually to be destroyed by the love of a dollar. Unchecked, money becomes our master, and we, its unwitting slave.

Arrowroot
The purpose of others

The arrowroot (also known as coontie) is a native plant of Florida and the Caribbean with the appearance of a small delicate palm. Its bulbous stem and roots have been used historically as a source of starch and flour. But first they must be washed or boiled to remove a toxin called cycasin, which causes terrible stomach upsets when ingested.

However, cycasin is not a problem for the Atala Hairstreak, a rare butterfly that feeds almost exclusively on the arrowroot. The butterfly lays its eggs, rears its larvae, and develops into adults on the plant, all the while subsisting on that perilous diet. The poison-engorged butterfly is thus well-protected from would-be predators, and to warn them, it sports a bright red-orange spot on its abdomen along with other flashy colouring that serves to say "keep away". In return for its food and protection, the Atala Hairstreak pollinates the arrowroot.

Sometimes we observe things that we don't understand – be it poison in a plant, or a perceived contrariness in the heart of a person. But that person may exist for a particular purpose that we cannot appreciate. It may take someone specially equipped to work with the individual and reveal that purpose without being harmed in the process. Someday, you may be called upon to do such a work.

Catnip
Be happy wherever you are

We have two cats. And they love catnip – anytime, anywhere, and in large handfuls. One munches on it, while the other buries her face and rolls around in it. They are reacting to a special ingredient called nepetalactone, which elicits very different reactions in different cats. Sniffing, licking, chewing, head shaking, chin and cheek rubbing, head rolling, and body rubbing are some of the behaviours. But not all cats are attracted – it depends on a genetically inherited tendency. In humans, catnip can help to induce sleep, but in some people it acts as a stimulant. (And nepetalactone can repel and even kill certain insects.)

It's hard to believe that one plant can produce such a plethora of effects. But how one responds – or if one responds at all – is so dependent on the individual. Think about the places you have been or have lived. For any given place, some will love it, others will hate it, some will be bored by it, and the rest will have no opinion. Busy cities are believed to be stimulating by some, lonely or dangerous by others. Some people find positives wherever they go, and their attitude is reflected in the faces of those who call that place home. Catnip of a kind is offered in many places – it's up to us to choose whether we will delight in it.

Olive
Do it right

The oil of the olive tree comes in different quality grades. Extra virgin oil is premium quality, extracted mechanically from the fruit in a very pure form. Virgin or plain olive oil may be derived using heat extraction or chemical methods that speed up the process but often produce an oil of inferior character. These lower grades are not as rich in nutrients and health-giving properties, and consequently, are not nearly as valued.

Choosing a path for convenience and speed is usually a recipe for mediocrity. The things that most enrich our lives usually demand a bigger investment of time and discipline. That investment eventually yields fruit that both nourishes and endures – a truly premium quality product.

Trillium
Something of value

In the rich moist woods of east-central North America, there resides a proud and majestic wildflower with three petals of pure white and deep green triangular leaves. The trillium is a lovely sight, honoured in the Province of Ontario as its official flower.

It takes a trillium at least five or six years to produce that flower, and up to fifteen years if conditions are harsh. Having to wait so long for seed, it's not surprising that the trillium takes the business of seed dispersal seriously.

The seeds are spread by ants, and are designed to attract these creatures. The seeds sport a special appendage called an elaiosome, a white oil-containing structure about the same size as the seed. Ants are enthralled by an elaiosome chemical that mimics the blood scent of prey insects. The ants bore holes into the trillium fruit to get at the seeds, which they then spirit away to their nests some distance away. Their larvae feed on the nutritive oil, and the seeds are deposited in the soil where they later germinate. The trillium has used a bit of ingenious trickery, but the ant profits well from it.

Clever devices are often used today to get us to buy something or accept someone's ideas. Sometimes they turn out to be nothing but empty promises. If you wish to win faithful customers, give them something of real value. They will then scatter the seeds that will expand your enterprise.

Logwood Tree
Wisdom

The tropical logwood tree produces a valuable natural dye called haematoxylon. This deep purple stain is extracted from the heartwood of trees felled when they are about 10 to 12 years old. The wood is steamed, boiled, or simply soaked in water.

The dye is used for tinting silk, fur, leather, wood, and cotton products. But its most valuable application is in biology. Scientists use the dye to stain cells that will be examined under the microscope. Haematoxylon is able to reveal the details in these cells as no synthetic dye can.

In its way, haematoxylon helps the scientist to discern truth, in this case about cell characteristics. We, too, need to discern truth – a different kind of truth – in our everyday lives, and in finding purpose for our years. For this, we must have our own equivalent to haematoxylon.

Wisdom is a great discerner. It reveals the true nature of the world around us and the secret places of the heart. It contrasts right and wrong. It is infinitely more precious than power and wealth. It is a great gift, for which there are no worldly substitutes.

Mangrove
Thrive in any situation

There is a tree that keeps a "foot" in both land and water, making perfect use of each. It is the mangrove, a tropical-coast species which can create dense forests. The mangrove lives in an unusually salty environment – a killer for many plants – and manages it well. That's because its roots are adept at filtering out salt – so good, in fact, that a thirsty traveller can have a drink of fresh water directly from a mangrove's roots, despite the salty surroundings. The mangrove also protects the adjacent land by preventing erosion and counteracting pollutants.

I admire the mangrove's knack for balancing its two worlds of land and sea. It makes the best of each, filters out the bad parts, and helps to keep the neighbourhood clean and healthy. We too can thrive in whatever environment we find ourselves, by looking for ways to work with the materials at hand, and by filtering out contaminants such as fear, worry, and doubt. As we succeed in our challenges, we can share that success by helping others to overcome their own hardships.

Tiger Lily
What's your backup plan?

Even though they're a bit on the weedy side, I love tiger lilies. Their perky orange flowers are a welcome addition to our August garden, where they have multiplied deliriously over the years since we planted only a handful. They grace the space near our front veranda, where we sit and enjoy them, as do the hummingbirds and bees. I'm amazed at how many new plants appear each year – hundreds, it seems – not just in their allotted spot, but in the nearby lawn too.

Tiger lilies are remarkably adept at reproducing themselves, using four routes to new plant production. Bulb offshoots (bulblets), bulb scales, seeds, and even aerial bulbils – little black nodules that appear where each leaf meets the stem – are all able to regenerate a brand new tiger lily. In fact, it seems that there's very little that could stop these tenacious tigers.

Versatility and variety – words that aptly describe tiger lilies. They have truly mastered the art of the backup plan. Have you?

Sugar Maple
Transform your colours

While out on my daily walk one September, I noticed one or two sugar maple trees in the neighbourhood starting to take on the red hues of autumn. Not the entire tree, but the odd branch tip here and there – typically those facing the sun. In a few short weeks, virtually all the leaves would be transformed to brilliant red, orange, or gold, but the early changes are usually rather piecemeal.

Readiness for change commonly develops in this piecemeal fashion. I'll notice first one thing in my life, then another, that no longer fits, and these small pockets of discomfort eventually grow and coalesce into a general longing for change and improvement. Transformation is necessary, if we are to prepare for the future. It is imperative, if we are to display our most brilliant colours.

Water Hyacinth
Staying power

The water hyacinth is a delicate-looking lavender flower that multiplies to produce a river of shimmering beauty, its colours shifting from lavender to purple under the changing skies. Its delicate appearance, however, masks a virtual indestructibility.

In the bayous of Louisiana, history attests to this fact. Many unsuccessful attempts were made to curb this invasive plant which threatened to smother the ecological balance of the area. Dynamite, sternwheeler-mulching, arsenic, and even flame-throwing were tried, to no avail. The hyacinth withstood them all, and continued to multiply. Even tornadoes and hurricanes, which destroyed other plants, only served to spread the seeds of the water hyacinth. Eventually, the herbicide *2,4-D* helped to bring the renegade plant under control, but only to a degree. The plant continues to outlast generations of humans as well as natural calamities. As one source put it, the water hyacinth is the survival flower.

What is its secret? Water hyacinths get their staying power from a canny investment in seed production. One plant can produce 65,000 others in a single season. An acre of flowering hyacinths may contain anywhere from 50 million to 800 million seeds, 95% of which stay dormant and can germinate any time within the ensuing 20 years.

The story of this obstinate plant may be telling us that the seeds we sow today should be of a lasting nature – not just prolific – their viability withstanding the ravages of time. They should emerge undiminished when it is right to do so. Anything less means we've undervalued our lives.

Gonyaulax Algae
Don't pigeonhole people

onyaulax is a type of dinoflagellate algae responsible for the famous red tides – massive algal blooms that kill marine animals. During red tides, fishes and other sea life die from lack of oxygen, while shorebirds, whales, and many other marine animals may be harmed directly by toxins in the algae.

Interestingly, *Gonyaulax* toxins may also be useful. One of these, saxitoxin, may be effective in treating nerve and heart disorders, and might also be useful as a local anaesthetic. Another feature of some *Gonyaulax* species is that they emit a beautiful glow, or bioluminescence, which is why they – and many other dinoflagellates – are known as the "living lanterns" of the sea.

Gonyaulax appears to be a paradoxical mix of the good, the bad, and the beautiful. But I think it's not much different with people, for we too have many aspects that are best appraised in context. Let's not pigeonhole people. Instead, we should be willing to look more closely at their various facets. We may be pleasantly rewarded for our trouble.

Vine Grape
Let your gifts blossom in stressful times

Grape growers have always been careful to time their harvests so as to avoid damaging or killing frosts. But one year, winemakers found out by accident that an untimely frost can bring sweet surprises. They discovered that an early November frost could help to concentrate the sweetness of the grape by freezing the fruit's water, which could then be separated from the remaining syrup using industrial processes. The concentrated syrup yielded a fine wine which became known as Ice Wine, now a valued – and expensive – specialty item cherished by wine lovers.

It is interesting that stress, such as frost, can produce such a wonderful outcome in vine grapes. I've observed the same principle at work in many people, for whom an untimely job loss, a health challenge, or a new responsibility, spurred them on to unique accomplishments. It is in the hard times, often under stress, that people learn how to concentrate and develop their gifts, and to resist dilution from panic and anxiety.

Mexican Jumping Bean
Unforeseen events

A delightful plant is the well-known Mexican jumping bean. Its autumn fruit is sometimes bored into by a moth larva which can't seem to stand still inside the bean, its motions producing the famous "jumping" phenomenon. An undisturbed bean stays put, but an inhabited bean goes places!

Unforeseen circumstances sometimes invade and disrupt our lives too, causing us to jump in new directions, often much to our dismay. But surprises – even alarming ones – can be a great impetus for getting ourselves out of those comfortable ruts and ditches that we sometimes settle into. Surprises can be the catalysts for real progress.

Acacia
Protection

The wood of the acacia tree is much admired for its strength, durability, and beauty. It was a prominent wood in biblical times, and may have been the wood used in the Old Testament Ark of the Covenant. It's a premium wood because of its great resistance to damage and destruction.

Some Acacia species use an ingenious strategy to fend off damage by enemies. The tree allows colonies of stinging ants to set up house in its spiny, swollen thorns. In exchange for a home and nourishing nectar, the militant ants attack other insects, herbivorous animals, and even people who threaten the tree. The acacia can be assured of safety, without having to do anything to protect itself.

We are told there is something that we can hold in our hearts that protects us unfailingly: God's promises. If we keep these dear, and nurture them with thoughtful consideration and application, they can be an unbeatable army against any adversary.

"I will never fail you or forsake you." *Joshua 1:5*

Pioneer Lichens
A charitable heart

Some types of lichen act as pioneers. For example, in areas where volcanoes are prevalent and lava-strewn rocks are the only thing left on the landscape after an eruption, not much can survive – except for certain pioneering lichens. These lichens use their fungal member to run little threads into the rock face, thereby anchoring the lichen securely. Then, the fungal partner produces special organic acids that dissolve the rock. The lichen actually feeds on this rock, leaving behind a pocket of soil when it dies. By creating soil from rock, the lichen prepares the way for other plants and animals to survive in those places.

These pioneers illustrate that it is possible to meet our own needs, yet simultaneously prepare the way for others. That's what happens when we offer charity – be it a gift or donation, a sympathetic ear, or a readiness to forgive. Most charitable acts cost little in comparison to the pockets of peace they create – not just for another, but for ourselves as well.

Prairie Lupine
You don't have to be first

Prairie lupine was one of the first plants to establish itself following the devastating volcanic eruption of Washington's Mount St. Helens in 1980. A short-lived perennial herb, it managed to establish itself quickly on the pumice plain left by the volcano. It did so through a combination of prodigious seed production and root-bacterial partnerships to capture nitrogen from the nutrient-depleted soil. Its pioneering spirit allowed it to flourish and influence the subsequent fifteen years of plant succession.

While growing vigorously, prairie lupine keeps out competitors because it grows so densely. But when it dies, it leaves behind a rich substrate in which other species will thrive.

There is a tendency to resent others who arrive on the scene before we do, seemingly getting the best of the markets, most of the profits, or credit for a discovery. That's the wrong way to look at it. Pioneers usually leave behind a legacy after they have done their work – a legacy that benefits those who follow and provides a rich medium for fresh ideas, new developments, and sometimes even greater contributions.

Duckweed
Accomplishments

Hailed as the smallest of flowering plants, the duckweed is a tiny aquatic dweller whose plant body may measure no more than 1/25 of an inch across. The smallest species of this group have no roots and produce minuscule flowers and fruit under 1/50 of an inch in size. That fruit weighs as much as a grain of table salt: four billion times lighter than a large world-class pumpkin.

Yet the tiny duckweed is capable of mighty feats. A carpet of it on the surface of a lake absorbs heavy-metal contaminants, and cleanses excess phosphorus and nitrogen wastes from runoff in farm areas. Duckweed incorporates these substances into its body's biomass, thereby helping its population to expand. When the duckweed population grows too large – threatening to steal light and nutrients from other vegetation – the tiny plants can be skimmed off.

When you're small – be it in size or stature – many avenues may seem closed to you. You may downsize your dreams, trim your expectations, or undervalue your contributions. Don't fall into that trap. You can accomplish wonders through focus and persistence. Over time, the fruits of your efforts will multiply to yield a luxuriant carpet of achievement.

Witch Weed
False friends

Found mainly in Africa and Asia, the witch weed is a parasitic plant that attacks food crops such as sorghum, millet, maize, and sugar cane. Once it sprouts, the witch weed has only a few days to live unless it can find the nearby root system of another plant. The weed sniffs out chemical signals, searching for potential plant hosts. When it locates a candidate, it infiltrates the victim's roots with an attachment organ. It then proceeds to live quite happily at the host's expense, feeding the host with hormones that will cause the host roots to multiply greatly, at the expense of shoot growth. The victim lives, but cannot reproduce. Meanwhile, the witch weed's needs are completely satisfied.

What at first appears to be a friend – or even a soul mate – may be just the opposite. Be wary of the individual who tries to exert control over you. It may appear that you are benefiting in some way, but it may be at the expense of something else that maintains the right balance in your life. Be discerning, and avoid becoming an unwitting victim.

Quiver Tree
Solitude

The quiver tree grows where other trees refuse to tread – in the very hot and arid regions of South Africa. Native to Namibia, it is known for its propensity for solitary existence. But occasionally these trees amalgamate into a forest. The Quiver Forests are an eery sight, with trees sparsely gathered into a surreal prehistoric-looking landscape – a forest of individuals, sharing a common place.

The quiver tree has adapted to the harsh heat and dryness of its home by storing great quantities of water in its trunk. Inside, the wood is very light and spongy. As the trunk and branches can be easily hollowed out, they were used as quivers by the indigenous San people to carry their arrows, making this species very useful to these bush tribes.

A solitude-loving tree that is both useful and able to live alongside others can serve as an example to us. Those who prefer the peace and quiet of being alone should nonetheless offer companionship to others as opportunities arise. A penchant for solitude does not mean we can't be useful to others, if we permit them to share the inner sanctum cleared by our times of reflection and learning.

Clusia
Take the first step

Seeds sprout in the ground, right? Well, the habits of the clusia may surprise you. Parrots and other birds that feed on the fig-like fruit of this tropical forest plant tend to drop the seeds right onto the tree canopy as they whizz by overhead. There the seeds germinate, the young sprouts living off nearby dead leaves or other useful debris high in the canopy. Only when this food runs out, the clusia extends tentacles down into the ground and begins vigorous growth.

If you wait for perfect conditions before you do something, those conditions may never come. Sometimes you have to take the first step in confidence and simply do what you can – even if you can't see, touch, or smell the ground. Use what you have around you to sustain you in the early stages, and trust that in time your roots will find a firm footing.

Elephant Tree
Create your own tapestry

Deep in the Sonoran Desert of Arizona and in Mexico lives the unusual elephant tree. A short tree with stubby limbs and grey, dry-looking leathery bark, the elephant tree would not impress many. Its short, stout, tapered trunks and branches look somewhat like elephant legs and trunks, hence its name. One learned author, writing of its value, said that it was another useless plant, without anything of economic value for man or beast.

But don't tell that to the southwestern native desert cultures. These peoples have always respected the elephant tree, using it in their healing and cultural traditions for many centuries. Used in incense because of its pungent eucalyptus-like fragrance, and as a remedy for coughs and other ailments, the elephant tree was an important member of the medicinal cornucopia of these cultures. Even today, some western practitioners use it in clinical practice to help combat herpes, cystitis, and various infections.

Others may say that something or someone is useless. That doesn't make it so. Few can fully appreciate the capabilities of another. Accordingly, we should never let others define our potential or sketch our future – their vision is too limited. Why settle for another's rough sketch when we can have a full tapestry of rich colour enlivened by our own fancy?

Saw Palmetto
Diligence matters

The emerald sunburst frond of the saw palmetto is a familiar sight in parts of the American southwest. Many know it as a healing herb, with benefits touted against prostate ailments and other ills. Whether or not the claims for healing are valid, it is a fact that the saw palmetto itself is quite a survivor.

The saw palmetto is particularly good at recovering from fire damage. Although its highly flammable leaves quickly burn to a crisp when fire rages through an area, it retains strong rhizomes (underground stems) intact beneath the soil. Calling on their supply of carbohydrates for energy, these rhizomes spring into growth at the first opportunity – even breaking out of winter dormancy early. Flower and fruit production are put on temporary hold while the leaves are regenerated. A plant that is burned in November can produce a large fan-shaped leaf by January. Plants from an entire burned area can recover fully within a year.

The saw palmetto is a diligent plant. Steady and sure, ready to move into action even when it may be expected to only rest. Diligence is a trait that moves us all to action, even when we're weary and bruised. It has saved many, enabling them to fashion the all-important first leaf in the frond of recovery.

Trembling Aspen
It's only a breeze

I love to watch trembling aspen when the breeze stirs its leaves. Dangling like a thousand silver dollars suspended on strings, the leaves quiver and rustle with the slightest provocation. I always expect them to fall off the tree, as they appear so precariously attached, but fast they hold even through the wickedest wind.

Sometimes it's easy to feel like those leaves – as we tremble in the face of an unsettling event. But don't we often surprise ourselves, finding that we can hang on until the gust subsides. And upon reflection, it's frequently true that what appeared to be an unrelenting gale was merely a breeze, rustling us to our very best.

Yellow Gentian
A bitter pill

Yellow gentian is a bitter plant. It is also a handsome plant, with erect stem and clusters of bright yellow blooms. It occurs naturally in the subalpine regions of Europe and Turkey, usually in hard, stony places. Containing bitter chemicals with names like gentiopicrin and amarogentin, the taste of which can be detected even when diluted 50,000 times, gentian contains some of the most bitter substances known to man. It has even been used as a scientific standard for measuring bitterness.

The plant is used widely in commercial "bitters", as it is reputed to increase appetite. It is an ingredient in many proprietary medicines, and is considered to be very useful in treating digestive disorders. In the Middle Ages, yellow gentian was used as an antidote to certain poisons. In all cases, to avoid risk of toxicity, only minuscule doses of the bitter compounds are used.

Bitterness is not a trait we normally prize. In a person, even a trace can do much damage. A bitter person poisons his or her environment rather than serving as an antidote, and curbs our appetite for friendship. Bitterness is best reserved for the plant world. In people, such a tendency is best rooted out.

Pine
Good health

Pine cones could hold a secret to protecting the human brain from cellular death induced by strokes. After a stroke, the body's brain cells go into overdrive to deactivate what they perceive as a damaging attack. But that can cause more harm than good if the neurological system over-reacts and destroys too many of its own cells. Researchers have found that certain tannins from plants can inhibit the enzyme in the body that initiates the damage, thereby saving the brain from harm. Gallotannins, as they're called, can be found in pine cones (and certain other plants), and extracts from these may be the basis of future treatments to help combat the effects of stroke. But to have significant benefit, these medicines may need to be administered within minutes after a stroke.

Sometimes, our body can seem to be our own worst enemy. But that is what happens when our physiological scales are tipped too far in one direction and balance is lost. Unless we take fast action to re-establish harmony in the body, we suffer, sometimes fatally. Let's not wait for a catastrophic event to galvanize us into action. Seek to achieve a balance today – by eating right, staying active, and getting enough rest. And don't forget the great powers of prayer, faith, and a mellow constitution.

Coffee
Guard your defences

If it wasn't for coffee and the caffeine jolt provided by each cup, a lot of folks would never get going in the morning. But I like mine decaffeinated. I buy the best quality decaf beans I can find, freeze them, and grind them fresh for each cup.

Decaffeination is done with "green" coffee beans, before roasting and grinding. A common method is to soak the beans in water, which removes the caffeine, along with some important flavour and aroma components. The caffeine is then extracted from the water using one of various agents (such as charcoal or chemicals) and the water containing the aromatic goodness is returned to the beans prior to drying and roasting. A fairly complicated process!

Why not just breed some coffee plant varieties to be caffeine-free? Well, some scientists believe that caffeine may be a key defence against feeding insects. It may even help the coffee plant to compete successfully against other plants because caffeine, being water-soluble, diffuses from roots into the soil and is toxic to various insects and fungi. So it could be catastrophic for coffee plants to be denied caffeine.

Like coffee, each of us possesses special attributes that help to protect us from harm. But sometimes we allow these to be dissolved away, perhaps through a lack of self-esteem or encouragement. Don't allow anything or anyone to dilute the potency of your personal integrity or character. These are vital defences in the struggles of life.

Hemlock
Freedom to grow

A walk through the lush rainforests of North America's Pacific Northwest reveals some intriguing finds. One of my favourites is the sight of hundreds of tiny western hemlock seedlings adorning the surface of a fallen log. These seedlings get their start from the nourishment and support of that log, which nurses them from its decaying body. As the seedlings grow, they eventually root in the soil and are then able to satisfy their own nutritional needs.

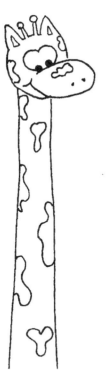

Hundreds of years later, one can see several towering trees in a row, maintaining the original alignment from the nurse log, their magnificent trunk bases still hugging the shape of a log that has long since disappeared.

We never forget where we came from, and who nurtured us. We were shaped by their influences – good and bad – so many years ago. Sometimes we use them as excuses for a life gone wrong. But, no matter how compelling these excuses may seem, we need to remember that we are now our own person – free to grow even beyond the confines of a disappointing childhood. This is true freedom.

Galdieria sulphuraria
Go where your gifts lead you

Among the red algae, there is one known as *Galdieria sulphuraria*. It inhabits hot springs bubbling at temperatures that would cook most other plants. In addition, *Galdieria* can tolerate very acidic conditions, surviving even in concentrated hot sulfuric acid and using hydrogen sulphide as an energy source. Truly an amazing plant. Scientists have found that these single-celled plants produce specialized stress-protective chemicals called polyamines which safeguard the integrity of their cells in these extreme conditions.

G. sulphuraria goes where no other plant can. It beats the odds under seemingly impossible circumstances. It protects itself from harm through chemical ingenuity. In short, it defies what we might expect from the average plant.

Don't let anyone tell you that what you aspire to do or be is impossible. You *can* go where others have not ventured. You *can* survive the extremes. You *can* maintain integrity of faith, spirit, and well-being in the face of great challenges. Your gifts are unique – who is to say where they can lead you?

Red Mangrove
Working and waiting

Tropical storms are notoriously savage in areas like the Gulf shores of Florida. Such storms can chew away great expanses of beach, eroding the shoreline by as much as a hundred feet. Ravaged too are the many plants that had settled on the site – plants such as the red mangrove. These trees are destroyed, only to be renewed by seedling sprouts alighting on the edges of the eroded beach. Later, the dense roots of the growing trees trap sand and debris from the tides, creating new soil and gradually extending the shoreline back out to sea.

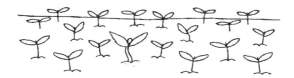

The red mangrove is a pioneer. It colonizes a hostile place by working with the barest materials to fashion a new home. It creates a fertile soil for future dwellers through skill and patience. It teaches us that if we are to carve out new territory, we must be prepared to both work and wait. A good deal depends on us and our ability to do certain tasks – but much depends on ebbs and flows beyond our control. Work to prepare yourself, while awaiting the tide that will solidify your efforts.

Goldthread
Digging for gold

Forests are treasure troves of fine woodland flowers. One such example is the goldthread, a plant with delicate star-shaped white blossoms that measure about 1/4 inch across. But to behold the real beauty of the goldthread one needs to probe the soil gently with a finger. Revealed will be a long thread-like root the colour of pure gold. Therein lies the exquisite magic of the goldthread.

At face value, something we do might appear good and satisfactory, and we may be content with that. But what untold treasures may be coaxed to appear if we are only willing to dig a little deeper. A good thing may indeed turn out more wonderful than we could imagine. So let's not stop at the surface – that's only the first line of the story.

Red Pine
Tempting scars

Many trees of the American and Canadian north woods will face fire at some time in their lives. A very intense fire kills trees, but a less intense one can partly burn trees and leave scars to mark its passage. Red pine is one of many species subject to scarring from low-intensity burns. The fire scorches the inner bark – or cambium – from which all stem growth initiates. When a section of that cambium burns, pitch or resin quickly seals the wound until new bark is formed – a process that can take years.

Interestingly, fire scars are more likely than unscarred tissues to be burned and re-scarred by future fires. This is partly because the resin coating is quite flammable, and because, even though the wound has been healed over, its new bark is thinner than that elsewhere on the tree. These scars become the tree's weak spots.

We each have our own weak spots too. They may be visible as the scars of former temptations which, like the tree scars, tend to leave us vulnerable in particular areas. And each of us tends to be susceptible to the same temptations over and over again, ones that seem to have our name stamped upon them. Succumbing to temptation may not destroy us immediately, but it weakens us and leaves us more vulnerable to the next attack.

Soybean
Fuel the spirit

How would you like to ride a bus powered by soybeans? That's what they're doing in Cedar Rapids, Iowa. Buses traditionally fuelled by diesel are getting a breath of fresh air with the introduction of biodiesel fuel made from soybeans. It seems that soybean oil produces very clean energy – hardly any smoggy particles to clog the lungs, no carbon monoxide to pollute the blood, nor sulphur to acidify the air. And it works just as well as smelly old petroleum diesel. The soybean oil is combined with methanol in the presence of a suitable catalyst, and – *Poof!* – clean diesel.

Clean fuel to whisk travellers about town – I like that. Now if only we could challenge our bodies to run on clean fuel, and steer our minds with wholesome invigorating thoughts. How much healthier for everyone our world would be.

Lavender
Our choice

When I think of lavender, I envision genteel elderly ladies with their perfumed talcs, bath salts, and toilet waters. It was a favourite of our grandmothers' generation, and of many generations before that. The Victorians loved its sweet fragrance. The ancient Romans, Egyptians, and Arabians used it for many things: embalming the dead, bathing, cooking, and as insect repellant. As recently as World War II, it was used to disinfect hospital rooms. Today, people appreciate lavender for its soothing and calming effects.

Lavender is grown in many countries, its nature as diverse as the locale, from the sweetness of Provence lavender to the strong camphoric quality of the Dutch variety. Lavender oil is a mix of about 180 different components which produce an unrivalled complexity. Yet, for all its splendour, it is a plant that thrives on neglect, and once established requires very little water. In my own garden, I've dug it up, left the whole thing out for days while I contemplated transplantation, then plunked it back into the same spot – and the plant has continued to supply me with lovely aromatic blooms in spite of it all.

Sometimes the finest qualities are bred in the face of neglect. For instance, where someone who has had none of life's advantages (and few of its necessities) rises above circumstances to bless others. Someone who has asked nothing and received little, but who readily gives in myriad ways. Such a person shows that we are the ones who choose to become victims or victors.

Snowdrop
Ahead of the crowd

I n the latter part of winter, when snow still covers the ground, there is one flower that blooms. It is the snowdrop. With tiny greenish white bell-flowers and grassy leaves, it pops out of the ground with a spunk that belies its fragile stance. That such a small flower can brave the chills and lashings of winter's last breaths is nothing short of wonderful.

In the 19th century, Hans Christian Andersen wrote a tale titled "The Snowdrop". The story vividly tells how excited Sunbeams welcomed the snowdrop and said,

> "Beautiful Flower! How graceful and delicate you are! You are the first, you are the only one! You are the bell that rings out for summer, beautiful summer, over country and town." However, the Wind and Weather said, "You have come too early. We have still the power, and you shall feel it, and give it up to us. You should have stayed quietly at home and not have run out to make a display of yourself. Your time is not come yet!"

> But the flower had more strength than she herself knew of. She was strong in joy and in faith in the summer, which would be sure to come, which had been announced by her deep longing and confirmed by the warm sunlight; and so she remained standing in confidence in the snow in her white garment, bending her head even while the snowflakes fell thick and heavy, and the icy winds swept over her.

The story then compares the snowdrop to a certain poet who came *too early, before his time, and therefore he had to taste the sharp winds.* And so it is for others who dare to step out ahead of the crowd, who despite having to face biting criticism, confidently chime their bells of hope. Like the little snowdrop, they too can triumph.

Cacao
Don't lose heart

I love chocolate in all its forms – from creamy rich bars, chunks, and truffles, to silky cocoa beverages. And I appreciate the hard work that goes into the making of these sublime confections. In Trinidad, earlier generations of my family produced chocolate for their livelihood.

It all starts with the tropical cacao tree, whose large fruit pods must be harvested and opened to extract their 50 or so cacao beans. The beans are then dried, toasted, hulled, crushed, and flavoured. In the old days, crushing of the seed was done with a mortar & pestle and lots of elbow grease. Dry-looking cacao seed particles, after much painstaking pounding, would eventually reach a point where they would simply coalesce into a creamy mass, as the cocoa butter contained in the seed centre did its lubricating work. From this point, one could shape chunks of dark solid chocolate which, when hardened, could be grated and boiled with milk to provide a frothy, nourishing drink.

The work of patiently pounding cacao seeds is not something most of us have time or inclination for today. Machines now spare us many such labours. Yet those times come when we find ourselves grinding away at a project or task but making little obvious progress. Then, just as we think we've reached our wits' end, suddenly it all comes together, and the pieces that previously appeared disjointed harmonize and blend into a delightful outcome. Sometimes success takes only a little more effort – so don't give up too soon!

Lantana
Flattery is no compliment

The lantana is a garden or greenhouse shrub with flowers of pink, white, orange, or yellow. Used sometimes in American garden borders, it seldom grows taller than three feet. But it's a different story in Hawaii, where the lantana is not a native but an introduced plant. There, the warm, nourishing climate brings out a ferocious growth in lantana, with the shrubs reaching ten feet tall, the stems bearing vicious thorns, and the plants trouncing the native species. It's not a welcome plant there, but it is too late. Much damage has already been done by this otherwise modest species.

Modesty and flattery are enemies. If you would have one, you should ignore the other. Flattery is unusually fertile ground – it irrigates egos, feeds arrogance, and nurtures the spores of greed. It is not a natural growing environment for most of us, and in it, we can become something of a monster. While a sincere compliment is a blessing, empty flattery can be a curse.

Wheat
Real nutrition

Wheat is one of our most valuable plants. Rich with nutrients, the wheat grain yields some of our most satisfying foods. Until recent times, the entire wheat grain was ground between two stones, but since the latter part of the 19th century, wheat has been ground by mechanized steel rollers that take away the bran (the nutritious brown coat) and the germ (or embryo). Further processing produces a low-nutrient "refined" white flour – something that has far less food value than its original product.

But we have now come to appreciate the goodness lost in modern methods, and many have returned to the original stone-ground process to retain the richness of the wheat grain. Whole-wheat products are now popular again.

Our modern world is so good at cultivating abundance. Great flowing fields of wheat are a commonplace sight. But while we sow bountifully, we may reap foolishly. Along life's walk, we often settle for refined white flour rather than insisting on the bran and the kernel that give meaning and substance. Scrutinize the path that you're taking – make sure it has real nutrient value.

Aloe Vera
Healing

Aloe vera is the healing plant that many of us keep on our kitchen window sills. Famous for its ability to mend wounds and burns, a little snip of its fleshy succulent leaf is all that is needed to protect and heal a small accident. It has been used since ancient times to fight infection. Scientists don't fully understand the mystery of aloe vera's healing abilities but it appears to have something to do with improving oxygen supply to the skin and encouraging the formation of new tissues. Whatever the secret, it's an ancient remedy that is as popular today as ever.

Healing of the body is a marvellous process that involves the expulsion of destructive invaders and the formation of new tissues. Healing of the mind is similar. Its recovery from wounds also requires cleansing and renewal – cleansing of fear and distress, and renewal of strong new fibres of resolve – the kind of healing aid that doesn't even take space on your window sill!

Douglas Fir
Lifestyles

In the Pacific Northwest, the Douglas fir has great stature. It yields more timber than any other tree in North America, and is one of the best timber producers worldwide. Douglas fir occurs as two distinct varieties: coastal and inland. The coastal variety is a magnificent tree, and is the timber giant of the two. It thrives in mild, moist conditions, where it can grow to 250 feet tall and six feet in diameter, and live more than 500 years. The inland variety, on the other hand, is hardened to a tougher existence, ready to withstand dry, cold interior conditions. There it grows more slowly and is much smaller than its coastal cousin.

Two very different lifestyles, and it would seem the coastal variety has the much better deal. But its existence is not without challenge. All that moisture creates a favourable environment for root rot disease, a great destroyer of this coastal king.

People are quick to compare their lifestyle with that of another. And often we feel ourselves falling short of another whose comfy existence seems replete with life's perks. But where you are today may have little to do with where you'll be tomorrow. And comparing your lifestyle to that of another is futile because you do not know that person's full situation. While your struggles may be more visible, another's may be hidden but equally hard.

Cinnamon
The spice of life

Most of us appreciate the heavenly scent of cinnamon. Whether it is used as cinnamon bark, powder, or oil, there is no fragrance or taste quite like it. My favourite is the homey aroma of cinnamon-spiced apple pie, but I also love cinnamon-laced potpourris and bark ornaments tied up with brightly-coloured ribbons. At Christmas time, our kitchen is suffused with the perfume of cinnamon – from hundreds of our favourite baked goodies.

Cinnamon comes from the bark of the cinnamon tree, which is found in certain tropical locales. The best quality cinnamon – a fine light reddish-brown product – comes from Sri Lanka and Indonesia, and possesses a perfect balance of the volatiles cinnamaldehyd, eugenol, and a few trace components. Lesser quality cinnamon is found in other regions, and tends to be a darker colour, coarser in fragrance, less pure, and more bitter in taste.

The quality of cinnamon depends not only on where it is grown but on the skill of the bark peelers – individuals who have honed their talent over many years – who coax the prized inner bark from the twigs of the cinnamon tree. Their efforts produce fine long "quills" or pipes of bark, expertly stripped from the twig.

Through history, cinnamon has been prized by peoples far and wide. We are fortunate indeed to be able to enjoy this lovely spice. It brings an exotic treat right to our home, and flavours our day with the rich ancient history and talents of many cultures. You may not be a world traveller, but the world can visit you right at your table.

Daffodil
Beauty can be poisonous

Daffodils are the trumpeters of spring. Their bright yellow blooms herald the start of a new season, full of promise and renewal. But with this beauty, there is a dark side. Daffodils contain toxic alkaloids and other bitter substances that, if ingested, can harm or even kill a human being.

It's not hard to mistakenly eat a daffodil bulb. The sprouts look a lot like those of common onions. A daffodil can establish itself in an onion patch or other part of our garden, looking like a harmless wild onion – and these rogues have been eaten by people who thought that's exactly what they were.

Daffodils are delightful as long as we consume them with our eyes rather than with our mouths. Similarly, many of life's pleasures can be relished with proper use, but they can prove deadly if devoured without restraint.

Arabidopsis
You are a masterpiece

Plant scientists are excited about a recent milestone in research. They have identified all of the genes in a mustard-like flowering weed named *Arabidopsis*, making it the first plant to have its genome completely sequenced. Genes make up the blueprint for all the characteristics of a plant or animal, and *Arabidopsis* has over 25,000 genes. It has taken many years of work to get this far, but the real work still lies ahead.

The challenge is to work out what each gene does for the plant. The experts say it will take at least another ten years – and I believe that's optimistic.

Meanwhile, the human genome is also being unravelled, and its nature is much more complex. Who knows how long it might take to understand precisely what each of our genes does, or how they work together. Perhaps plant genes will tell us something about our own genetics – that remains to be seen.

One thing is clear: There is a vast difference between describing something and understanding it. Life on Earth is intricate and miraculous in its design, and its deepest secrets may never be revealed. If we are ever tempted to think of ourselves as mundane, let us remember that each of us is truly a miracle of accomplishment and an abiding mystery. Our blueprint has yielded a masterpiece.

Inky Cap Mushroom
Choosing your livelihood

Mushrooms have strange and unique qualities. Take the inky cap mushroom which grows in grass or on decaying wood. It is a charming little fungus with a grey-brown cap resembling a partly closed umbrella. As the mushroom matures, the cap turns inky black, hence its name. But that's not the strange part. The inky cap is an edible mushroom that is normally quite harmless – unless you make the mistake of drinking alcohol with it! Some species of this group contain the chemical coprine, which disrupts the normal metabolism of alcohol in your body, even up to several days after eating the mushrooms. The result can be a rapid buildup of toxins, producing stomach upset, facial flushing, nausea, heart palpitations, and other disturbances.

Unhealthy combinations are always best avoided – whether it be mushrooms and alcohol, or people and situations. For example, some personalities are better suited to certain kinds of livelihoods than others. The methodical, unhurried thinker should not pursue a fast-paced, on-the-edge career. Conversely, the high-energy, lightning-speed problem-solver would shrivel in a sedate job. Your livelihood should not clash with your disposition. It's just not healthy.

Lichen
Litmus for life

Many people are familiar with litmus papers, those little pH indicator strips that turn either red or blue when dipped in acid or alkali. Litmus papers are imbued with special dyes derived from several species of lichen.

In modern times, the *litmus test* has been used in a philosophical sense as well. We may say something is a litmus test of success, or love, or commitment, meaning that it is a discriminating test that will produce a definitive answer.

I wonder how many of us would be willing to subject our priorities to a litmus test. What if we chose peace of mind as our litmus, and held it against each of the priorities, large and small, that we hold at this very moment. Take a few moments to run the test, and see what doesn't pass. Perhaps these are burdens we shouldn't be carrying.

Resurrection Fern
New life

One of the plants adorning trees in the Florida Everglades is an epiphyte known as the resurrection fern. Epiphytes attach themselves to a foundation but draw all of their nutrients from air, rain, and sun.

The resurrection fern is a rather dowdy-looking plant when it is dry, exposing only its brown underside to the curious eye. One might unwittingly assume that the plant was dead before the rain. But after a life-giving downpour, the plant transforms into a lively bright green.

Many people believe in another kind of regenerating food: Jesus Christ. He called himself the bread of life – offering new life, and providing sustenance in the face of hardship. He promises to enrich us with the gifts of His spirit, today and forever.

Kerosene Grass
Unwind

In the Australian Outback lives an entertaining weed called kerosene grass, so named for its extreme inflammability when dry. I've heard that an old Outback trick is to remove one of its tiny stem-like fruits from a clump, moisten its base in one's mouth, then stick it partway into the sand. Right away it begins to twirl, slowly burrowing its seed base into the ground and firmly planting itself.

A clever system accomplishes this trick. The germinating fruit is a cone-like structure sheathed in a hard coat. Three strands, or awns, emerge from its top, wound together in a spiral column. When the base is moistened, the springy strands relax and untwist, causing the small fruit below to rotate – a rather ingenious way to re-seed itself after rain.

Spinning helps this grass to establish itself. People, on the other hand, often find they are dizzy from lives spinning out of control. Lives that are overly complicated, bound up with tension and twisted by worry. The establishment of the kerosene grass comes from unwinding and release of tension – that is how the seed is planted into solid ground. So, instead of spinning to tighten the tension, let us focus on unwinding to release it.

Blueberries
Encourage the best in others

Plump, juicy blueberries taste great and are also good for you. They're loaded with anthocyanins. These impart the blue colour and are thought to act as important antioxidants – powerhouse chemicals that sponge up certain toxins in the body – a big health plus for those of us who love to eat these luscious blues.

But the secret is to eat fresh berries soon after picking. Within about ten days, the berries can lose half of their antioxidant strength. Alternatively, the berries can be frozen immediately after picking to help preserve the anthocyanin content.

Similarly, contained within each person is a storehouse of potential which can degrade quickly if unused or mismanaged. If you wish to encourage the best in others, first take the time to understand them – their abilities, their priorities, and their weaknesses. Take an interest in developing and preserving their gifts – because the gifts of others can nourish many lives.

Balsam Fir
A timely friend

Balsam fir, like many forest trees, can't thrive without the benefit of some very important partners in the fungal world. Mycorrhizae, as the tree root-fungal partnerships are called, help the tree to better acquire nutrients from the soil, while also proffering food and other benefits to the fungus.

Each tree species has a favourite fungus, but the favourite may change, depending on the environment. For instance, a fungus that works well with the tree in the shade may be too demanding and costly a friend in bright sunshine. So the tree switches to another type. Choosing the right partner for the situation involves finding one that is beneficial but not a drain on the tree's resources.

Of course, people also need the right partners. We may look more to one friend or another, depending on the situation we're in and what a particular friend has experienced. One person may provide a special blessing here, another there, so you should treasure the diversity of your friendships.

Ohia Lehua Tree
Grief calls for feeder roots

So much can be learned from plant pioneers such as the ohia lehua tree. This Polynesian tree can be found growing in a most unlikely place – the small cracks formed by hardened volcanic lava. Feather-light seeds alighting into these crevices sprout and settle in, able to do so only by virtue of their very shallow roots. Such shallow root systems, while a disadvantage in hurricanes, are just the ticket for making a home in lava cracks. Over time, the roots grow strong and start to spread the crack wider and wider, making a much more receptive environment for other plants to move in.

The loss of a special loved one can leave us feeling desolate – as if we are wedged into a tight, suffocating crevice of grief. The walls seem to close in, and, for a while, it's all we can do to make it from day to day. During this time, recovery doesn't come from exploring the deep philosophical nature of death, nor from quickly immersing ourselves in a new enterprise. It comes from extending our hands to friends and caring for our daily needs rather than working through the complex details of the future. It comes from gradually enlarging the space around us so we can breathe. We rely on a temporarily shallow root system – feeder roots rather than sinker roots. The sinker roots come later as we become stronger, even able eventually to reach out to another grieving soul.

Bristlecone Pine
Secrets to long life

The bristlecone pine can live for several thousand years. One might expect such a long-lived tree to be quite regal in appearance, but the bristlecone in its advanced years is straggly, squat, and gnarled, with many dead branches. Beauty – by conventional standards – loses out to character, and therein lies the bristlecone's secret to long life.

This tree grows slowly and deliberately, producing tightly-packed growth rings that yield a durable, decay-resistant wood. The tree also gets by on very little food, water, and energy, and even allows parts of itself to die back to conserve precious resources. It protects itself from pests by producing the necessary chemicals to fend off attack. And, bristlecones do not live in isolation but thrive in communities of other plants and animals, all affording mutual benefits.

These aspects of the bristlecone's character may reveal some secrets to a long life for us too – such as take your time, don't waste your resources, protect yourself from destructive influences, and share your life with others.

Cashew Tree
Deactivate the poisons

I'm a cashew nut lover. I can't resist the smooth rich flavour of these delicious tropical treats and I don't mind over-indulging when I get the chance.

When I was little and lived in Trinidad, we had cashew trees in our backyard. The nuts grew at the base of the cashew pear, which is edible and tasty. But whereas one can eat the pear right from the tree, the nuts must first be carefully detoxified – by roasting to deactivate toxic oleoresins in their oil. (Oleoresins can cause severe dermatitis and other allergic reactions.) With the poisons destroyed, the nuts can then be safely consumed.

To find the treasure in a situation, we may have to manage poisons that also reside there. Poisons may take the form of troublesome individuals, a lack of confidence, or circumstances that seem to conspire against us. But these toxic elements can be overcome through determination, integrity, and patience. In this way, we can be assured that our labours will produce a worthwhile harvest.

Hammer Orchid
Don't settle for substitutes

Some plants are notorious tricksters. The hammer orchid of Australia mimics a female wasp in appearance, managing to fool unsuspecting male wasps into believing they are mating with the real thing, when in fact, they are just helping to pollinate the flower. The male wasp appears about two weeks earlier than the female. He sees the hammer orchid, whose floral parts resemble and even smell like the female wasp, and alights on the flower, whereupon he is promptly clubbed by a spring-loaded lever which catapults him into the pollen. After a bit of bumbling around, he emerges, stunned but bearing a lump of pollen baggage, ready for delivery to the next orchid. And on it goes, until the female wasp finally appears and climbs onto grassy vegetation where he can see her. Once he sees her, the hammer orchid has no further chance of capturing the wasp's attentions.

It's easy to fritter our energies chasing what appears to be right for us. It's so tempting to go after the first thing that catches our eye that we don't think to wait and see what may be just around the corner. When the right thing does appear, we may miss it. Unlike the wasp and the hammer orchid, who eventually manage to satisfy both their needs, we may not be so fortunate – and we may end up paying a high price for our haste and poor judgment. Make sure you're going after the real thing.

Buttonwood
Simple spunk

The buttonwood is a salt-forest tree which is named for its groups of little round fruits and flowers. Found in certain hurricane-prone areas, it's not unusual to see a big buttonwood tree that has fallen over many times, yet has managed to bring itself upright each time. The trunk may lie recumbent for a time, grow horizontally, and even double back upon itself before growing skyward again. It doesn't give up until it is pointed in the right direction and back on its way. Now, that's spunk!

Being knocked down time and time again can be discouraging even to the hardiest of people. But there is much to be said for simple, stubborn spunk. It refuses to be beaten, and it helps us to find our way again. Sometimes we have to retrace our steps, or even lie low for a while. But that's better than giving up and letting the hurricane defeat us. If a tree can do it, so can you.

Horsetail
Abrasive types

Every spring and early summer I wage a losing battle with horsetail weeds in my rock garden. After a little rain they pop up with a vengeance, spreading underground rhizomes and sprouting shoots everywhere that demand space from my flowers. I pull at their jointed stems but it does little good, as they just break off at the soil level and continue to proliferate underground.

Although I've seen little to praise in the horsetail, others have put it to good use. In ancient times, the Romans used horsetail to clean pots and pans, and the silica in the stems even rendered these vessels non-stick. In the Middle Ages, it was used as an abrasive by cabinetmakers to clean pewter, brass and copper, and for scouring wood containers and milk pans – hence, its alternative name, scouring rush.

Irritating, abrasive, stubborn, and intrusive. These nicely describe horsetail to my mind. Unfortunately, they also apply to a few individuals that I've met. The kind of people who just rub me the wrong way, but whom I can't seem to get away from completely. Of course, viewed from another angle, I probably seem exactly the same to some folks. Now, in my own case, I'd like to be given the benefit of the doubt, so it's only fair that I should do the same for another. After all, we just might find something to appreciate in each other.

Turtle Grass
A peacemaker

Turtle grass is the most abundant seagrass in the Caribbean. Forming vast underwater meadows of broad ribbon-like leaves, it feeds and shelters sea life and helps to stabilize seabed sediments. It breaks the force of waves and slows down currents, all the while releasing rich nutrients to sustain plants and animals. This simple grass is vital to the health of the sea.

It's like that with some very special people. They stabilize their environment with a peaceful attitude, they nurture others with sympathy, and they break the forces of dissension with wisdom and humour. They cultivate a meadow of serenity in a sea of disquietude. To be such a person is a great thing indeed.

Spanish Moss
Beauty that endures

A familiar sight in the bayous of Louisiana is the Spanish moss, which cascades from the limbs of large swamp trees, giving the bayou its ghostly gossamer quality. But the beauty, softness, and fragile façade of the Spanish moss mask an indomitable character that perseveres through time.

The Spanish moss isn't a true moss in the botanical sense. It is a member of the pineapple family, and it is an epiphyte, which means it simply uses the tree for support and is nourished by air – literally fed by dust and other nutrients brought by rain and wind. It can grow on a dead tree just as well as on a living one. No helpless beauty here, but a real survivor that flourishes without even a root to call its own. Little surprise that Spanish moss is the stuff of legends.

James J. Kilpatrick wrote of Spanish moss as a metaphor for its native region: "An indigenous, indestructible part of the Southern character; it blurs, conceals, softens and wraps the hard limbs of hard times in a fringed shawl."

Beauty that truly endures cannot exist alone, but abides alongside self-sufficiency and perseverence. These meld the delicacy of gossamer with the foundation of finely-honed steel.

Forests
The path to maturity

Forests are always changing. It might not seem so to our eyes because we tend to appreciate change most easily in short spurts. But the forest changes gradually, often over hundreds of years. For instance, a northern forest after a devastating fire starts out with virtually no life. Within a few seasons, new tree seedlings arise from light-loving species such as jack pine, birch, and aspen. Gradually, other tree species make their appearance – red or white pine, and others that don't mind being in the subtle shade of existing trees. Finally, as the forest approaches maturity, the spruces and firs settle in. These rather like the shadows, eventually producing a deep, dark canopy and what we know as the climax forest. We prize mature forests for their soothing character, their protective solidity, and their stately beauty.

I have known a few elderly persons whose lives have traced a similar path. In youth, they basked in the limelight and grew strong and confident. By mid-life, they had learned to champion the needs of others, turning the spotlight away from themselves. In their later years, their quiet assurance and sound wisdom sheltered and comforted others in turbulent times. To reach that state is to realize true maturity – which exists in the restful shade of a blessed spirit.

Partridge Pea
Sensitivity

The partridge pea, a prairie wildflower, is a little on the bashful side. Its bright yellow flowers, although lovely and cheery, often remain hidden among foliage. And its compound leaves – up to 25 pairs on individual leaflets – usually fold shut when touched. Sensitive to significant disruptions in its growing environment, the partridge pea may also be especially vulnerable to climatic changes.

Such sensitivity is common in our world. They may be the shy, cautious individuals with little confidence and few friends. They may be the gifted artists who use their talents to reflect life's hues and tones. They are the quiet observant ones, whose thoughts are revealed only to those who undertake to seek and listen. It is easy to ignore and even trample upon such people. Don't do it. Take the time to listen to the one who speaks quietly – the one whose sensitivities sweep as brushstrokes of colour and insight across life's canvas.

St. John's Wort
Inside and outside

S t. John's Wort is a wildflower to be reckoned with, as any insect predator soon finds out. Tempting in appearance, with its little yellow blossoms and perky aspect, the plant has little problem attracting lots of curious insects. But if one feeds at the banquet provided by its pretty flowers, a bug's satisfaction is unfortunately short-lived. Contained in the harmless-looking blossoms is a nasty chemical, hypericin.

Hypericin, gobbled up with the blooms, travels through the insect's digestive system, eventually ending up in the outer body layer. There, it reacts with sunlight, in a manner most unfriendly to the insect. Toxic products thus formed target insect proteins and nucleic acids that are vital for survival, deftly destroying them and killing the insect.

The things we accept into our bodies and hearts rarely remain there. They permeate our system and eventually emerge in the outer layers of our personality, where their effects are laid bare for all to see. Then we must face the reactions of those we respect. But we have the choice of whether to absorb that which is positive, truthful and uplifting, or that which will ultimately condemn us when held up to the light of day.

Candlenut Tree
Light your own candle

The official state tree of the Hawaiian Islands is known as the *kukui*, or candlenut. From this tree comes a grey-black nut about the size of a walnut, with a bony shell and an oil-rich kernel. The Hawaiians used to burn the kernels for illumination. They would string them in a row along the tough midrib of a long coconut leaf and lean the leaf upright against a stone. The nut at the top would be ignited and it would burn for several minutes – just like a candle. Then, as the oil dripped down, the next would light itself, and so on in cascade fashion for as long as light was needed. Even today, some old-timers speak of a light bulb as an electric *kukui*.

Modern times have given us many conveniences and gadgets. At the mere flick of a switch, we have instant everything. We even become complacent about it all. But what about our own creative spark? Within each of us there is a rich kernel of creativity just waiting to be ignited. And there's no end of outlets for its expression. How infinitely more satisfying to bask in the glow of our own candle than to linger in the shadows of another man's dream.

Oat
Recovering from setbacks

When oat plants get knocked over, they have a way of righting themselves and growing vertically again. The plant produces a messenger chemical, inositol triphosphate, that announces within the plant that it is flat out and needs to straighten up. After a while, cells begin to elongate on the underside of the pulvinus – a swollen joint on the stem where leaves are produced. This one-sided elongation bends the stem upward to resume normal growth.

Note that once it is down, the plant takes time to assess its situation before it expends any energy – after all, it may just be momentarily swayed by the wind. But when ready to act, it activates specialized parts to execute the recovery. It doesn't lie there and give up, nor does it wait for external remedies. The oat contains within itself the resources to evaluate and change the situation.

If you've been knocked down by disappointment or failure, it is important to realize that you can recover and continue to grow. Give yourself time to assess the situation. Avoid blaming others. Then galvanize the special abilities that you have been blessed with to aright yourself – you'll find that you have the resources for just such times.

Wasabi
Create a niche

If you're a fan of Japanese cuisine – like my husband and me – you are probably familiar with wasabi, the pungent green condiment used to complement raw fish and noodle dishes.

Wasabi spice comes from the plant of the same name. Wasabi is a rare and hard-to-grow species that inhabits the cool mountain valleys of Japan, where its roots and thickened underground stem are fed by a steady flow of stream water. Oddly, wasabi thrives when its roots are flooded. Where it has been coaxed into cultivation, growers have to raise wasabi in gravel beds next to streams. Gravel and waterlogging – not the stuff one usually associates with vigorous health.

But wasabi has a secret. Contained in all that flowing water is a rich supply of oxygen, which aerates wasabi's underground parts and enriches them with substances acclaimed for their healing properties. Wasabi is a master at using what would suffocate most other plants, in a unique way to benefit itself – and us! That's how one creates a thriving niche: by inhabiting the surprising, unusual, and often-rejected corners of life in imaginative and productive ways.

Cap Throwing Fungus
Don't call it simple

Fungi are simple plants. Or are they? Consider the cap throwing fungus, a cunning mushroom that has mastered some ingenious ways to spread its reproductive spores. This mushroom has a built-in light tracking system that bends to follow the sun's movements. Then, using its internal clock, it throws its spores at 9 a.m., aiming at an area likely to be open so that passing animals will help disperse them further. The fungus waits until it is angled just right to maximize the dispersal area. As an added touch, the spores are coated with glue to adhere to the travellers. Rather sophisticated, I think.

It's tempting to think of certain things or people as simple. But the plant world reveals that few things are as simple as we may first believe. We do ourselves and others a disservice when we fail to appreciate the ingenuity of others. Perhaps they know something that we would be wise to heed. Maybe right now, someone is looking to cast their favours in your direction – so take the blinders off and look around.

Sugar Cane
Sweet experiences

People of the tropics have long enjoyed a special treat – the sugar cane that grows so well in those areas. Sugar cane plants have toughish stems that are rich in sweet juice, and when the canes are cut, many a child (and adult!) has had the pleasure of chewing and sucking on the fibrous sticks. I relished these myself – the sheer pleasure of biting into a fresh firm cane, and the lingering sweetness contained there.

Of course, there are mechanized processes of sugar extraction – such as those that crush the harvested canes in large roller mills similar to the old-time wringers used to squeeze water out of laundry. The sweet juice that gushes out and the cane fibres are then cleaned of dirt with slaked lime, and boiled down to syrup. Eventually, sugar crystals are separated from the "mother liquor" by spinning in a centrifuge that operates somewhat like a spin-dryer for clothes. The sugar is further refined into what we use in our kitchens.

Mechanized production, albeit more prolific and sanitary, can't match the pleasure of getting the juice out yourself from that simple little stick. Maybe there were a few bits of dirt in my cane juice – that was all part of the experience. All I know is that sugar never tasted so good and, I imagine, was never so full of nutrients. Experiencing things is like that – a little time-consuming, often slightly dirty, yet savoury and worth it.

Freesia
Creativity cannot be rushed

In my mind, there is no other flower with a fragrance as wonderful as the freesia. A native of mild South African climes, freesias are popular bulbs in North America, where they brighten dark winter days with their beauty and rich perfume. Resplendent in shades of sunshine yellow, purest white, or intense gold, freesias remind us that spring is not far away and winter isn't so bad after all.

I've looked everywhere for an extract or even an artificial scent of freesia that captures its fragrance – without success. These imposters are either too flat, too sweet, or too simple. So I have to be content with a few days or weeks of its charm, and then wait patiently until the next season.

Freesias can be a joy to grow indoors and can provide a good supply of cut flowers. But one must observe an important rule: When the flower stems have formed, don't snip a branch until the first flower has opened and shows colour. Otherwise, they will not open sufficiently in water. Everything has to be ready and ripe for bloom – this is not a plant to be hustled along.

A freesia bloom is like a fine creative work. It cannot be rushed, but has to unfurl in its own time and in its own way. It cannot be duplicated. And once complete, it cannot be surpassed.

About the Author

Gina Mohammed is a research scientist, speaker, and writer who has shared the extraordinary world of plants with scientific and popular audiences for over 20 years. She enjoys learning not just about plants but from them as well.

Dr. Mohammed holds a B.Sc. in Biology from the University of Toronto in Ontario and a Ph.D. in Plant Physiology from Simon Fraser University in Burnaby, British Columbia. After her lengthy career as a research scientist and with over a hundred publications to her credit, Gina now runs her own consulting company.

Gina lives in Sault Ste. Marie, Ontario, with her husband, Dan, and two plant-devouring cats.

About the Artist

Nathalie Gagné is a talented young Québec artist, age 12, who has already won prizes for her work. Nathalie lives with her family near Montreal.